Kanpur: 1857

Niall Moorjani

methuen | drama

LONDON • NEW YORK • OXFORD • NEW DELHI • SYDNEY

METHUEN DRAMA

Bloomsbury Publishing Plc, 50 Bedford Square, London, WC1B 3DP, UK
Bloomsbury Publishing Inc, 1359 Broadway, New York, NY 10018, USA
Bloomsbury Publishing Ireland, 29 Earlsfort Terrace, Dublin 2,
D02 AY28, Ireland

BLOOMSBURY, METHUEN DRAMA and the Methuen
Drama logo are trademarks of Bloomsbury Publishing Plc.

A catalogue record for this book is available from the British Library.

A catalog record for this book is available from the Library of Congress.

ISBN: PB: 978-1-3506-0014-0
ePDF: 978-1-3506-0015-7
eBook: 978-1-3506-0016-4

Series: Modern Plays

Typeset by Mark Heslington Ltd, Scarborough, North Yorkshire
Printed and bound in Great Britain

For product safety related questions contact
productsafety@bloomsbury.com.

To find out more about our authors and books visit
www.bloomsbury.com and sign up for our newsletters.

This version of Kanpur: 1857 was performed at the Pleasance Theatre as part of the Edinburgh Festival Fringe from 30th July–24th August 2025 and was supported by the Charlie Hartill Fund.

www.pleasance.co.uk

PLEASANCE THEATRE TRUST

Since 1985, the Pleasance has stood at the centre of Fringe theatre and comedy. With an international reputation and a network of alumni that reads like a Who's Who of contemporary performance, the Pleasance is a home for daring new voices and experimental work.

Operating both as a major festival organisation – hosting twenty-seven temporary venues across three Edinburgh sites during the Edinburgh Festival Fringe – and as a year-round theatre and artist development centre in London with two permanent spaces, the Pleasance fosters creativity at every stage.

Our London and Edinburgh operations are entirely symbiotic, working together to nurture talent across the UK and beyond. A registered charity in England and Wales since 1995 and in Scotland since 2012, the Pleasance is dedicated to creating opportunities for artists throughout the year.

THE CHARLIE HARTILL FUND

The Pleasance's flagship fund offers unique and unparalleled support to artists through direct cash investment, programming and mentoring support. Through the fund, we hope to remove the financial risk for companies and allow creativity to take centre stage.

The fund was established in 2004 in memory of Charlie Hartill.

Author's note

Thank you for picking up a copy of *Kanpur: 1857*, it is a play about a topic which has endlessly fascinated and horrified me in equal measure for many years. It is a story which encapsulates so much about humanity in its toughest times, us at our best and worst with all the ethical complexity that comes with that. Whilst the play is often heavy in its subject matter, I hope the use of humour and satire lands well with audiences and I suppose readers as well. People will make what they will of it, but I consider all of the characters to be complex and nuanced, much like this moment in history. I don't really have much to say here but thought it important to mention that the play was written in response to three principle things: my own reaction to first reading about the Indian Uprising and the Kanpur Massacre, the lack of understanding about the topic in Britain and particularly Scotland (where I am from and a monument to the fallen highland soldiers still stands outside Edinburgh Castle, and the ethnic cleansing of Gaza in response to the events of 7 October 2023. Whilst this piece is a story about the Indian Uprising, it was written with a deep understanding of the parallels between what happened in 1857 and what is happening now. It shocked me as to how much a story from 150 years ago could feel like it was being played out moment for moment in the modern day. An oppressed people violently attacking their oppressor, the oppressor responding with horror and enacting collective punishment on the entire population in retribution. I also, I suppose, wrote in response to my own reaction to these moments. As someone who identifies as a pacifist I of course condemn all kinds of violence, but I thought it important to challenge my own hypocrisy of supporting and even heroizing the violent anti-colonial rebellions of the past (the 1857 Uprising and so many more) and yet feeling uneasy when confronted with violence in the modern day. I do not pretend to have stumbled on great and clear answers to these immensely challenging questions about the ethics of resistance. But I hope the piece will serve to historically inform conversation on subjects we must speak up on, and urgently, in a time where our freedoms of expression are being stripped before our eyes, it feels all the more important to exercise them as much as we can, while we can . . .

A note on the history

This piece was made with artistic license but also immense respect for this complex moment in history, I have used my training as an MA (with distinction from Birkbeck University) level historian to apply the same level of rigour as I would to any essay or academic work. The events that lead to and comprised the massacre at Kanpur are well documented and simultaneously shrouded in mystery. It is not clear why a gunfight broke out on the banks of the Ganges, nor is it absolutely clear why the decision was taken to execute the British women and children who were being held after they had cared for them for weeks. What we do know is that the moment was held up by the British, from whom most of our sources come, as proof of Indians (and more broadly non-white Europeans) being little better than animals and requiring brutality and violence to be ruled.

It is into this historically complex and ethically challenging moment that I have chosen to insert two fictionalised characters, that of the Indian Rebel and the British Officer. This gave me licence to play artistically and have the characters explore this period in a way that felt modern and fresh, whilst being routed in meticulous research guided by the work of far more qualified academics. All other characters named (Janpath the Jain aside) are real historical figures whom we know to varying degrees. The only historical character who I chose to explore a different backstory to is Hussaini, she is remembered exceptionally briefly as a lowly sex worker (our sources do not use this modern language), the physical enactor of the murders of the prisoners. It makes little sense that the orders would have been hers to give unless she was a tawaif (a highly skilled and well-respected courtesan), and it also (to me and many others) seems she would have been a perfect scapegoat for the British (who already saw tawaifs as morally repulsive). I have also imagined her as a Hijra (India's third gendered community), who also played roles at court which have been written out of history due to the British hatred of them. It was not common for hijras to become tawaifs, but I felt it important to reflect the way in which the hijra community has come to occupy much of the same space tawaifs do in India today. And also to imagine a historical trans sex worker as a powerful, dignified and brilliant person. Finally, it seems important to note that I have chosen the term uprising to describe the events of 1857 here. In the play it is mutiny, as that is what the British used, I respect that many Indians would call this the first War of Independence, however (in line with most modern academic work on the subject), uprising feels correct to me as this was neither a mutiny as the British had no right to be there, nor was it a War of Independence as the state that would become India was not yet formed in the consciousness of the rebels.

Acknowledgements

As is cliche, but also profoundly true, it takes a village to write something. I think this is even more prevalent when talking about plays and particularly Kanpur: 1857. The piece was written by me, but constantly found itself bounced off, reviewed by and endured by a myriad different people without whom it simply would not have come to exist as it does. First and foremost to thank is my incredible co-director and performer Jonathan Oldfield, your keen editorial eye and storytelling understanding has been literally invaluable, and I am so grateful you were keen to undertake this journey with me. I started writing the British Officer with you in mind and you have had a huge impact on his words, his perspective and his way of being, just thank you. To Sodhi, your musical genius has raised the show tenfold and it's literally just such a privilege to work with you. I can't really think who else I would have turned to bring these words and this world to life. I am also endlessly grateful to the team behind the stage, to Mohammed for your incredibly detailed and compassionate sensitivity reads, to Nikita for encouraging and challenging me in equal measure, Hussaini would not be as wonderful as she is without you. Emily for telling me that the work was publishable and being a huge cheerleader and fund getter for this project from the outset, and Alice who did passes of the early script alongside your endless professional editorial work.

Then of course there are the amazing team at Pleasance and the Charlie Hartill Fund to all of you thank you, with particular thanks to Jonny and Ella, it has been such a privilege to work with you both and I cannot wait to see where Kanpur goes thanks to your belief.

Thanks also go to the International Scottish Storytelling Festival and Creative Scotland for funding and showcasing earlier versions of the piece (with particular thanks to Daniel and Lauren who has always championed my work).

To Sian at Methuen/Bloomsbury, I am still a little in disbelief that you picked this up and wanted to champion it all the way to publication, it means the absolute world.

Finally, there are Julia, Kate and Matt from Birkbeck who opened my eyes to what history could be and how it could be told. To my wonderful wife Robyn, who endlessly puts up with me doubting myself and always pushes me to believe my work has merit. My dad and my grandpa, who brought me up with a knowledge of my Indian history and have always supported me in learning more. And of course my mum, who when all others told me I couldn't write or would never succeed as a creative due to my dyslexia, told me not to listen and to keep working hard. To keep dreaming. To all of you and so many more, from the bottom of my heart. Thank you.

Niall Moorjani – Writer/Co-director/Performer

Niall Moorjani is an LGBTQ+, neurodiverse, Scottish-Indian writer, theatre-maker and storyteller based in Edinburgh. They're the co-founder of Suitcase Storytelling Company. Niall's work combines mythology and history with diverse and progressive themes to create rich, modern performance with themes of hope, joy and kindness. Niall's work is firmly rooted in their Queer and BIPOC identities and is actively created for LGBTQIA+ and BIPOC communities. Niall has created theatre for organisations including Southbank Centre (*Grow,* 2023) and Penguin Random House (*The Very Hungry Caterpillar,* 2019). They're a regular performer at the Edinburgh Festival Fringe and have performed internationally at Tank Theatre, NYC. They have been described as a 'storytelling genius' by the Scotsman. They have an MA (with distinction) in Public History from Birkbeck University.

Jonathan Oldfield – Co-Director/Performer/Script Consultant

Jonathan Oldfield is an award-winning performer, writer and director. He trained at Bristol Old Vic Theatre School. He is a BBC New Comedy Award finalist 2024, co-creator of BBC Radio 4 series *Time of the Week*, which was winner of the 2024 British Comedy Guide Award for Best Radio Sketch Show. He directed the Best Newcomer at Edinburgh Fringe Comedy Awards 2024, *Joe Kent-Waters is Frankie Monroe: LIVE!!!* He also directed the multi-award-winning *Lorna Rose Treen: Skin Pigeon*, winner of the Dave Best Joke of the Fringe 2023. As a performer, he played Joydali in *Star Wars: Andor* on Disney+. Other credits include: Nick Mohammed's *A Christmas Carol(ish)* in the West End, *The Power* (Amazon Prime); *The Mosinee Project* (New Diorama Theatre).

Hardeep Deerhe – Tabla Player

Hardeep Deerhe, known professionally as Sodhi, is a highly skilled and captivating musician, composer and performance artist based in Scotland. With his diverse range of talents and limitless creativity, Sodhi creates captivating soundscapes that transcend boundaries and captivate audiences around the world. Throughout his accomplished career, Sodhi has embarked on exciting tours across the USA, Canada, India and Europe, leaving audiences amazed by his exceptional musical abilities. His recordings have received global recognition and praise, reaching listeners far and wide.

Nikita Gill – Dramaturg

Nikita Gill is an Irish-Indian poet, playwright, illustrator and actor who has the attention of 750,000 Instagram followers worldwide for her work. Her work offers a shift of perspective which centres women in both Greek and Hindu myth as well as folklore. She has given a TEDx Talk, spoken at every major literary festival in the UK and been shortlisted for the Goodreads Choice Award in poetry three times, the Children's Poetry Award twice and longlisted for the Jhalak Prize. Gill has written seven poetry collections and two verse novels.

Mohamed Tonsy – Sensitivity and Story Consultant

Mohamed Tonsy is a queer Egyptian writer and ceramicist. Formerly an architect and a triathlete representing the Egyptian Triathlon Federation, he completed a PhD in Creative Writing at the University of Edinburgh. His writing has appeared in *Mizna* and *Epoch Press* and was shortlisted for MFest's 2021 Short Story Competition. He is the author of *You Must Believe In Spring*.

Emily Ingram – Producer

Emily Ingram is a director, writer and producer. Directing credits include work for Traverse Theatre (*Tam O'Shanter: Tales And Whisky*, 2023); National Theatre of Scotland (*Squeezy Yoghurt*, 2020); international digital theatre project *The Show Must Go Online* (2020–1) and Southwark Playhouse (*The Grandmothers Grimm*, 2019).

As an assistant director, Ingram has worked with Kingshead Theatre and Seabright Live (*Trainspotting Live*, 2024); Lyceum Theatre Edinburgh (*How To Be Both*, 2022) and Pitlochry Festival Theatre (*Sophia*, 2021).

Ingram works regularly with Some Kind of Theatre to produce award-winning touring theatre and with storyteller Niall Moorjani to produce critically acclaimed theatre-storytelling productions (*Kanpur: 1857*, Soho Theatre, Scottish Storytelling Centre and Pleasance Theatre).

Ingram's debut, multi-award-nominated play, *The Grandmothers Grimm*, won Best Script at the USA National Women's Theatre Festival 2023.

Ingram has worked as a workshop facilitator and workshop assistant for organisations including NYU, Graeae and Tron Theatre.

Helen Coyston – Set Designer

Helen Coyston is a multi-disciplinary artist based in Folkestone. From a theatre background she works across set and costume design, workshop facilitation and prop, costume and puppet making.

Recent design credits include: *The Big Pitch with Jimmy Carr*, a podcast for BBC Studios; *Dracula: The Bloody Truth, Aladdin, Beauty and the Beast, Cinderella, Jack and the Beanstalk, The Snow Queen, Treasure Island, Stepping Out, Alice in Wonderland, A (Scarborough) Christmas Carol, The 39 Steps, Build a Rocket* (all Stephen Joseph Theatre); *The 39 Steps* (Theatre by the Lake/Stephen Joseph Theatre); *The Curious Rat* (Little Angel/Page One); *Noor* (Kali Theatre/Southwark Playhouse): *Macbeth/Twelfth Night, Crime and Punishment* (Leeds Conservatoire); *Habibti Driver* (Bolton Octagon); *Home, I'm Darling* (Theatre by the Lake, SJT, Octagon); *Operation Mincemeat* (New Diorama Theatre/Southwark Playhouse/Riverside Studios).

Rho Chung – Technical Operator

Rho Chung is an academic and arts writer. They are an American transplant to Scotland, where they completed their PhD in English Literature. Rho has forthcoming work on early modern trans studies and genderqueer Shakespeare casting.

Rho works as the theatre section editor for *The Skinny*, Scotland's largest arts and culture magazine. They also freelance as a director and dramaturg, focusing on stories of systemic violence and queer futurity. They are delighted to be involved in *Kanpur: 1857* amidst a cultural environment that stifles resistance and imagination. Another world is possible.

Kanpur: 1857

List of characters played by original cast

Niall Moorjani   **Indian Rebel**, *a storyteller who followed*
                  their lover Hussaini into rebellion against
                  the British and now faces execution for the
                  crimes of Kanpur
Jonathan Oldfield **British Officer**, *the officer tasked with*
                  interrogating the Indian **Rebel** *for*
                  information as to Nana Sahib and Tatya
                  Tope's whereabouts
Sodhi   **Musician**, *a tabla player who has been*
                  made to play to enhance the entertainment of
                  the trial/execution

List of characters in the Rebel's story

Hussaini: *a hijra and tawaif who advises Nana Sahib and is the inspirational revolutionary. Also the lover of the rebel on trial*

Nana Sahib: *Peshwa of the Maratha Empire and leader of the rebels at Kanpur*

Tatya Tope: *the right hand man and lead general of Nana Sahib*

Old Janpath the Jain: *a harmonium player who joins the rebels*

General Wheeler: *a British commander who surrenders to the Kanpur rebels*

General Havelock: *a British commander who 'liberates' Kanpur from the Indian rebels following the events of the story.*

Projection titles

1. *In the year 1857 hundreds of thousands of Indians rose up against the British in rebellion . . . They failed.*
2. *The ringleaders were strapped to cannons and blown to smithereens in front of crowds who were forced to watch.*
3. *Often these events were made into shows, with live music and entertainment surrounding the executions.*
4. *Audiences were forced to watch these shows. Consider yourself this audience, and a fictional prisoner will tell you a true story.*

Rebel *Strapped to a cannon.*

I was born in a village near Kanpur, northern India. We grew up by the banks of the Ganga, mother Ganga. I remember playing in the cool shade of the bayans by her banks. I loved how if you passed a seemingly quiet bush butterflies would burst out in a noiseless cacophony of colour. I remember standing. And watching. And waiting. Waiting for the bright blue and orange flash of a kingfisher. Burning all kinds of flame, hot and cold burning as one in a blur across the surface of the water, before disappearing up and into the trees. Have you ever caught a glimpse of a kingfisher after waiting for hours? It is perfect. OK, I wasn't the kind of child who could wait for hours. Seven minutes normally did for me. But when I did wait and I did see one. It was everything. I was never a good decision maker. I always struggled to know what to do. Like in the games, kabaddi and Gilli Dhanda, I didn't know whether to stick or twist so I always loved to just watch. So watching the kingfisher was so captivating, just by watching it felt like I was involved in some perfect little natural drama.

I miss those heady days by the banks of the Ganga, and as much as that is where my story most likely ends, it begins properly on the first day I went to a local market as a small boy.

It was too much for me at first. The smells hit me initially, the sweet smells of fruits, spices and cooking, all infused the hot air. There were colours, like the butterflies but in the fabric. I had never seen so many colours or so many cuts of cloth. Then there was the noise. Stronger in many ways than the smell was the noise, a heady din of hagglers, haggling over this and that, rat and tat. A Jain called Janpath played a new instrument from Europe, a harmonium he said, my mother said he was dreadful, but I was too young to know good from bad and loved it. His playing calmed me and I began to drink the market in like the finest chai and I must have been a funny sight. Jaw on the floor and eyes shooting in every which direction.

Then there was a sound above the sounds, a huge fanfare surrounded a figure on a horse. He was a white man. Not brown like me and my mother. His skin was like the goats' milk my sister and I poured into the chai pot, his eyes were blue like a clear winter's sky and his upper lip was flecked with hair that might have one day formed a moustache. He wore pale cream trousers and his coat was red. His rifle gleamed and shimmered in the growing sunlight.

The man began to speak and evidently he spoke well, no pauses or slips or stops. But it was in a tongue I did not understand. The gathering crowd we formed whispered Britisher, it hummed with excitement and fear. Then the word 'laggan' passed from his lips, but young as I was I understood that to mean tax. He was here to collect taxes on behalf of the zamindar. But this year they were to increase, in fact they were to triple. The whispers became mutterings, which turned to groans as he went on. The longer he spoke, the more men, all with red coats and shimmering rifles, appeared behind him. But still the mass of people spiralled each other into deeper discontent. My mother, always alert, pulled me away. But, just on the edge of the market, a sound that I had never heard rang through my entire body.

Later, I would see things like this many times, a British officer firing into the sky to disperse a crowd, but this time I turned and my mother tried to stop me, before she stepped in front, I know not whether to shield my eyes or look on in horror herself. There was something on the ground. It was the body of a child, not much older than I, not wretching or writhing just very still. A few people were hunched over them, too shocked to wail or scream, though I don't doubt those came later.

I looked then at the white man, a pistol being placed in its holster, and beginning to turn for the road which lead to the town. It was not like the stories, when a young protagonist

locks eyes with the villain and swears revenge. He didn't see
me and I didn't swear revenge. In fact, I never saw him
again. I didn't understand that my world, until that moment
had been one of banyan trees, kingfishers and butterflies,
now it was one red coats, bullets and bodies. And that was
the first time I saw a white man.

*A man dressed in a red coat who has been sitting in the audience
stands up and breaks the moment with clapping after a pause.*

Officer   Wow, that was great, really great, love the energy
and the lyrical language, really it's above and beyond. But I
am afraid that does not answer the question I asked.

Rebel   Yes it does.

Officer   No it doesn't.

Rebel   Yes it does.

Officer   Oh this is fun, bit of pantomime, ohh no it doesn't.

Rebel   Can't we just go through this as usual like with the
other officers? You say, where are Tope and Sahib? I say I
don't know. You hit me with something heavy until I pass
out and we do the whole thing all over again.

Officer   Sorry old bean, I don't do things that way. Much as
I cannot wait to hear where Tope and Sahib are. All that
nasty beating, it's just not my style. I'm a fair man, I want
both sides of this, ours and yours. Proper British legal
justice.

Rebel   You make it sound like our two sides will be treated
equally.

Officer   That is how our justice works. Two sides. But, one
story. One verdict. One truth. Fair. Anyway, why start so far
back? I wasn't expecting your literal life story.

Rebel   I felt you needed to see before, so you could
understand.

Officer   Why would you want to imagine things before the British, we are the best bit in any story about India.

Rebel   I find context is very important to answering big questions. Everything is a story we tell.

Officer   Ohh, that's a nice line, can I have that?

Rebel   What?

Officer   Everything is a story we tell. Feels delicious to say. I'll have it.

Laugh.

Officer   Why do you laugh?

Rebel   How can I not? Anyway, you have taken so much, what is a phrase?

Officer   Actually, your work could do with some levity. Don't get me wrong, I loved the lyrical language and the heightened style. But for a professional storyteller you are quite wooden. I expected more movement and hand gestures.

Rebel   Hand gestures???

Officer   Ohh yeah, that is my fault, ha, your hands are literally tied. I could do anything. I'm not going to hit you. As I said, that's just not my style. But I could do this . . . (*Takes out matches and lights one.*)

Rebel   No! No! God no, I don't want to die. Not like this. Not yet. Not . . .

Officer   Woah, woah, woah there my man. Well, this is progress. For a moment I was worried you were going to be one of those lunatic rebels that doesn't mind dying. I was only playing. No point in lighting the fuse just yet, (*Unties* **Rebel**.) there, enjoy the space, not like you could run too far, not with all the armed guards. They would kill you before you got a few feet away. Not like anyone can go very far anywhere until this ends. If you need the toilet you should have gone before.

(*Picks audience member.*) Specifically you, you look like the type.

Rebel   I cannot believe you gather crowds of my people to force them to watch this!

Officer   Oh come, isn't this entertainment at its finest? We cut down so many trees to make this space. Probably the same ones from your little prologue. How fitting and now here you stand. By the banks of your beloved Ganges. Everything is a story you say and we all have our parts to play. You. A defiant rebel who doesn't want to die and has a tale to tell. Me. A charismatic officer who needs answers. Even if they didn't want to watch I am sure they could hardly take their eyes off it.

Rebel   You treat me like a performing monkey? Am I a beast to you? Shall I bark my responses? Shall I whimper at your feet?

Officer   I have seen this so many times before. This is dull, you are dull. I was really hoping we could do something different with you. And it is so hot. Why is it so hot?

Rebel   The monsoon rains are late. They will come. And I hope they wash away your presence,

Officer   And will bring your long-awaited freedom, I know. Gosh, be less predicable, this isn't what I wanted. Look, if you are this angry the whole time it isn't going to be a very interesting hour. Relax. I untied you, didn't I? Trust me.

Rebel   You expect me to trust you?

Officer   Look, that tone is all wrong. I'm going to give you a minute to compose yourself. We'll do this my way or not at all. And then your story finishes. Unfinished. We want this to go off with the right kind of bang, don't we?

Officer *leaves.*

Rebel (*to audience*)   Is there any word of Hussaini? I must live to hear word of her? I cannot die until I know she is safe. Is there no word? Then forgive me. I will try to play his game.

Officer (*abruptly returns with a guitar*)   Now will you answer my questions.

Rebel   I was . . . I will.

Officer   Ooh, this is much more like it.

Rebel   Is that a guitar?

Officer   I was put in mind of a little wrinkle and tinkle when we had a musician on the cannon last night.

Rebel   A Jain musician?

Officer   Don't think his name was Jane. But he was useless, his fingers shook so much he couldn't play a single note. Been like that with a few of them, not sure why, they just buckle under the pressure of being strapped to a massive cannon . . . and then they make such a mess.

Rebel   Mess?

Officer   Ahh yes. The red stained sand is a little off putting, isn't it. That was a mess of his own making really. I really don't like it when the cannon goes off but I can only give so many chances before it becomes pointless. Fortunately, the blood will wash away with the rain you promise will come. Shame though, because I do love music. Ohh, Sodhi, begin please.

Officer *signals to a tabla player to start playing.*

Rebel   What are you doing?

Officer   Well, if you are really going to go for it, which I love, just to be clear. I thought what harm in having a musician throughout, you know, for them, modern audiences lose focus without multiple points of stimulation.

Rebel   Multiple points of stimulation?

Officer   Exactly. This will also help clarify elements of the narrative, whilst simultaneously enhancing its emotion and the drama.

Rebel   You are saying they will get bored of me telling the story of how I got strapped to this cannon unless Sodhi plays tabla.

Officer   Great, I am glad you understand. Now we seem to have reached an accord on your position, I really do wish to hear your story. Who knows, tell it well we may all get a happy ending.

Rebel   What does a happy ending look like to you?

Officer   I should be asking the questions, but that is a good one. Well, you tell me the tale in dramatic fashion. I come to know and trust you. You prove you weren't involved in the horrid crimes of Kanpur. You come to know and trust me. As an officer, I need you to give up the hiding position of Sahib and Tope. As a Christian, I need you to admit what your people did was wrong and condemn them. Then I get a Victoria Cross and hey, maybe you even get to go home. A happy ending indeed.

Rebel   I give you all that, and in return I keep my life?

Officer   Exactly, well, probably, hopefully, and you say we Brits aren't merciful. But first, the story. Ohh, I really do love it, all of this. Storytelling. Performance. Drama. Oh, my grandmother used to tell such tales. And I am something of a performer myself. Your story might be the only time we do something like this here. Might as well make a show of it all. And, go.

Rebel   We had taken Kanpur.

Officer   Before Kanpur. Kanpur happened during, I wanted before.

Rebel   The British had ruled us for near a hundred years. The Marathas defeated, Mysore defeated, even the mighty Sikhs, defeated, now the once proud Mughal rulers in name alone and bent double to serve the British. Taxes were rising. Our crops replanted with tea and opium, our people shipped across the world to replace slaves in the colonies. Our people being told they were lesser than the white Britishers who now ruled us . . . Our people . . .

Officer   So boring. I am not interested in a history lecture. Come on, give me the story. Think of it as a once upon a time thing.

Rebel   Once upon a time?

Officer   Yeah you know, once long ago around a campfire kind of thing. It would be a lot less dull. And this is all about other people. Talk about you, why did you become involved in the Mutiny?

Rebel   I hope not to offend, but it is very hard to tell, with your interruptions.

Officer   I just want you to get it right. Funny that, it is 'your story' but you need someone like me to make it work, I wouldn't keep interrupting if you had it right the first time. Clear?

Rebel   Crystal. Once upon a time, then?

Officer   Wonderful.

Rebel   Not so long ago, the child who played by the banks of the Ganga and watched the kingfishers fly grew up. Grew up in a world which was changing, the old powers had given way to new powers and they all moved in ways ever stranger. The child had learned that there was small merit in observing rather than doing. Especially when those observations were told as stories. Ohh, I mean, that is the best time to simply watch and listen. Sat around the fire with wise women telling tales of old kings and queens, and of folk heroes and of well, all of it. They, well, I decided the one thing I wanted to do was tell stories. So I learned as many as I could and started telling them. I was lucky, I wandered village to village with tales to tell and was given chapatti and daal in return, sometimes a coin or two. In walking, I saw so much of the country, dense green jungle gives way to wide planes, to fields and farms, waterfalls and lakes. I will never forget seeing tens of elephants simply wandering in the jungles which lie at the feet of the Himalaya. Nor bizarre, giant, white bats hanging in the moonlight of the Thar Desert from the walls of Jaisalmer. And sunset over the great heaps of boulders, stacked by the gods like marbles, in Karnataka.

Though tales of my tales travelled far and wide and eventually I found myself home, relief in being back I was now telling at the court of our Peshwa, Nana Sahib himself, Peshwa of the Maratha kKingdom. He loved to hear tales of Indian heroes like Lord Rama and Hanuman.

Ohh, the feasts we had, no longer did I eat chapaiti and daal alone, I ate kebab, mutton and chicken, naan bread straight from the tandoor and the a dal makhani which seemed richer than the princely states.

There I performed for Nana Sahib and his court. And so I performed to you Britishers, some would even speak to me after and slowly but surely English was taught to me. So I may share stories in your tongue.

I saw the way they spoke to Sahib, and to our most prized leaders, to his face they were nothing but courteous and behind his back the jokes they made.

But it was in his court that I met her. The one that began all of this for me.

Her name is, I pray that it still is, Hussaini. I still remember the first time I met her. She was performing at court for Sahib, the way she danced, the way poetry danced off her tongue and the way she spoke when the British guests were gone. Then, next time, it was by the banks of the Ganga, we sipped on chai as she spoke, the sun set as she spoke, a fire blazed and its embers danced . . . with the stars as she spoke and all of it seemed irrelevant.

Officer   Sorry, sorry, I really promise I won't interrupt again, what you are doing is great. So much better, but can we try again with a guitar, Sodhi. I just don't think tabla is right for this. Please can we, please?

Rebel   Must we?

Officer   Ohh, give it a go.

Rebel   Her name is, I pray that it still is, Hussaini. I still remember the first time I met her. She was performing at court for Sahib, the way she danced, the way poetry danced off her tongue and the way she spoke when the British guests were gone. It was by the banks of the Ganga, we sipped on chai as she spoke, the sun set as she spoke, a fire blazed and its embers danced . . . with the stars as she spoke and all of it seemed irrelevant. Because she was speaking. I was like a child listening to a story, my mouth must have been on the floor as she used words in a way I had never seen before. She spoke with such passion and such strength and such kindness. She wanted us to take back what was being taken from us. She wanted us to stand up tall for ourselves.

Her eyes blazed orange like the soil of the Deccan. Her mind was sharp. Her hair and clothes immaculate. Her voice like honey and saffron. I couldn't believe a person like her was real, so charismatic, so smart, so strong.

She wanted the British gone and knew that together we could make it happen. We fell to talking after and it turned out she liked stories.

I told her everything I knew, stories from the Mahabharata, Ramayana, high tales and low tales, those were the ones she liked the most. Stories of everyday people doing incredible things. One evening we hid by the banks of the river, away, the moonlight spilling silver all over the world and the midnight air hot, she kissed me. And I kissed her and in the warm midnight air and with her I felt like I could help put the world to rights. Because I would help her and the world would be right for doing so . . .

Officer   You fell in love with a revolutionary. So you followed her into the fray? Ha, our tremendous hero is a tremendous sap. Though, I am not heartless. Your story reminds me of a song. All about love and home. It sings of wild mountain thyme and heather. Very beautiful love songs and stories.

Rebel   I know that song.

Officer   Well, well, aren't you more surprising than a jack in the box that I thought was a Russian doll. How do you know it?

Rebel   There are a lot of you Britishers around, some of you like stories, one shared this song with me, it is very beautiful.

Officer *starts to sing 'The Braes o' Balquhidder' and is cut off.*

Rebel   If these are to be my final moments, I would really rather you didn't.

Officer   Sorry 'bout that, old chap. It is hard not to get swept up in a love story. The song makes me think of my wife who is no longer with us.

Rebel   I am sorry, I am sure she is in a better place.

Officer   Dundee.

Rebel   Dundee? Your word for your heaven?

Officer   Oh, no, that is a place. Sorry, she isn't dead, she just isn't with us in India anymore. She is back home in Scotland. The song isn't a British song really, it is a Highland song. Funnily enough, there is a story behind it. Please have a seat. Once the Highland peoples, or the Gaels were different

from the Scots. They had their own language and culture.
Clan chiefs were chiefs of the people rather than the land
and so the people were cared for directly by them. But that
ended after they lost a great battle to the British at Culloden
around a hundred years ago.

My grandmother used to become so quiet when she talked
about it, which she did rarely, the British forced her and her
family to leave their homes by burning it down. In fact, it
was her own clan chief who sold her out. Sheep were worth
more than people and profits ultimately do matter. Hard
time for her, my grandfather died defending his house. So
she was alone and on top of that Gaelic was made illegal to
be spoken and so was wearing tartan. She moved to Dundee
and worked in a factory. She tried to keep her culture and he
held it close. She had my dad. Then the only way you were
allowed to wear tartan was by joining the British army in a
highland regiment. So my dad did, this very regiment in
fact. The 78th Highland Regiment. And with his new social
standing he he married a more well to do lowlander and
well, here I am.

Rebel   With a voice like your oppressor and and a hundred
years later, doing to us what the British did to you. Seems a
strange way to live.

Officer   Look, it wasn't pretty. But it really is for the best.
The Highlands have never been more organised or
profitable for the country. Sometimes there is a price to
progress. Modernity has brought jobs, irrigation,
technology, science, reason and even the marvel of the
railway. We are going to be bringing those here soon, you
lucky devils.

Rebel   You are sure the Highlanders are lucky?

Officer   Trust me. Things are fine with the Highland
people now and we are celebrated as model Scots, our
culture is legal again. I can be proud of my heritage. I hear
that on the very esplanade of Edinburgh Castle they are

already planning to build a monument to our fallen brothers from this very conflict. May it remain there unchanged for hundreds of years.

Rebel   How lovely. If that works for the Highlanders, fair enough, but what's in it for us?

Officer   Look what your people have done. You would think that you were trying to throw off monsters. We are custodians. Civilisers. Modernisers, and it isn't just practicality, we are working to rid your country of the disgusting practices of your people, ones that even you must admit are wrong. Burning women whose husbands have died, having people you literally won't touch because they are impure. Not . . .

Rebel   I hear you. I do not support these practices either. But they are not so Indian as you think. How little you understand us.

Officer   How little you understand that we are saving lives. We are saving souls. Look, it isn't us forcing it on you. We are working with your upper class Brahmins on this, it is not like they don't have a say. What we are doing is collaborative, peaceful, it is progress.

Rebel   You call this progress? Did you not know that before you turned up we were one of the most celebrated civilisations on the planet. Your own travellers marvelled at this place when they first came. What makes you so sure you are right to change us.

Officer   Because this, all of it, has to be right . . . This is all part of God's plan. He is taking us forward until our final days. So everything that passes before then is all taking us towards a brighter future. Speaking of progress, we need to make some with your story. So, you fell in love with a revolutionary, what happened next? Your telling has been so much better, but can we think of a way of making it clearer with the names?

Rebel   Everyone hear knows of Tope, Sahib and Hussaini,

Officer   Look, I know they do. But anyone from my side may need some help. Now I know this is going to be a stretch but imagine that most people aren't Indian, in fact imagine they are white like me. How are they going to understand if you have all these figures they have never heard off, with names that sound a bit weird? I love the once upon a time feeling, maybe let's double down on that, like give each of them an epithet, Nana Sahib –

Rebel   The leader.

Officer   Tatya Tope.

Rebel   The general.

Officer   Hussaini, your lover.

Rebel   My light.

Officer   Great, whatever you like. But try it like that and let's see how it goes.

Rebel   And how should I refer to you? The British?

Officer   Ohh fun, erm, ooh, dealer's choice.

Rebel   How about the Giant.

Officer   I . . . love it. Strong, powerful, and giants are so often cast as the villain, I love a good retelling. Yes, the Giant it is. Carry on.

Rebel   It is true that for a brief time, in the early days of trade the Giant who had visited our shore had looked up to us. And our most powerful had enjoyed his presence in the country, at court, they liked the technology he brought and some of the ideas too. The world was shrinking and it was no bad thing.

But slowly and surely the Giant, suckled on the milk of our rulers, grew, larger and larger. And as he drank, our rulers were drunk by infighting. The Giant was wily as well as strong and before long the Mughals were rulers in all but name, and we knew that the Giant was in charge. Mostly because he wouldn't stop telling us.

Many adapted to this. We had adapted to the Mughals and many other rulers before the Giant. Indians, in fact, were needed for his great project of expansion across the country. In fact, Indians began to work for the Giant. We worked in his factories, his courts and worked most importantly in his armies. Some were treated well, some weren't. Despite attempts on both sides to get along, tension grew between us and the Giant. Those crops replaced led to famines. Taxes were raised and people became poorer. Preachers came from the Giant's country and told us we were a beastly people with beastly religions. When challenged with words often the Giant would respond with bullets. So we whispered of how we might throw off this new power, this Giant, but ultimately none of us thought it possible, he was too big. We, the people, were like a forest trapped in stifling heat, surely a blaze or deluge would change everything, but nothing changed.

Until one day. One day, a rumour spread amongst the Indian soldiers in the Giant's ranks. The sepoys. Word spread among them that you would ask them to use guns greased with pig and cow fat. Even you must have known that to ask Muslims and Hindus to do such a thing would go
. . .

Officer   It is a baseless rumour, we are actually very culturally sensitive to the lesser people.

Rebel   Of course you are. Some brave sepoys in Meerut refused to use their sacrilegious greased guns. And naturally, being so culturally sensitive the Giant put them in prison. Sentenced them to ten years hard labour. This was the spark, it erupted into flame, the prison stormed, the British officers killed, the sepoys saved. The sepoys marched on Delhi. A blaze. Soon what started with a few hundred sepoys turned into a few hundred thousand of us. Wildfire spread. News that this was our moment. Then Lucknow fell. Gwalior fell, Arrah, Bareilly. The whole of the north of India was falling to rebels, burned with the hope of freedom, with this mind we knew that even giants could be felled.

And then Hussaini, my light, she came to me, said she was going to fight and of course I followed her. Nana Sahib, the leader, was persuaded by her to lead us into battle, and like tributaries of some great river, we the many who wanted change, flooded to him. Within days there were fifteen thousand of us. Farmers, market sellers, merchants and peasants alike, we were all there.

And then all looked to a man on horseback, Nana Sahib, our leader, a man so clearly born into power. His moustache perfectly trimmed, his clothes bright and flowing, his horse proud and decorated and his hands soft. His sentences and speeches were long and poetic, stuffed full of Sufi references he had learned from Hussaini.

Next to him, also upon a horse, was Tatya Tope, the general. To see them side by side, you may have thought them similar men, same cut of cloth, same moustache. But two more different people there never were. A man of humble origins, Tope had become one of Sahib's best generals. His hands were hard. He did not like poetry.

And then I watched as Hussaini joined Nana Sahib on horseback and raised his arm aloft, Nana Sahib Zindabad, she cried, Nana Shaib Zindabad, long live Nana Sahib. Long live our freedom.

We laid siege to Kanpur for three weeks. The Giant's troops dug themselves in, but little fighting was needed as they wilted in the summer sun. General Wheeler, the Giant's man, surrendered. There was a lot of blood and the bodies of British officers, they lay there like white lilies severed from their stems. We gave them a day to bury their dead, but the ground being hard with summer many bodies were just left outside the walls. It was the first time I had seen a body since of the child at the market. Now it was white bodies killed by brown hands and killed by their own stubbornness, I don't know why they didn't surrender earlier. I wish I could say it didn't bother me, that they had chosen this life. But some of them looked so young.

Considering there had been relatively little bloodshed it was very easy to be swept up in celebration. We leapt like children celebrating the first rains.

We had fought for our freedom and here it was, within the city high walls and we marched straight to the palace, which Wheeler had used as his headquarters. Imagine it, so many of us from farms who had never seen such a sight. It was a beautiful building, all high pearl white walls, wide dreaming windows. Bright green banyan trees growing in the courtyard. A breeze flew through and nearby was a deep well still full of cool water.

We were the masters of our destiny, masters of Kanpur. There was just dizzy high conversation, we were giddy on what we had achieved.

Hussaini declared that we must feast and Nana Sahib threw his hands up in noble agreement. A feast was cooked, so bright in colour, the orange of the daal, the ruby red chicken, the vivid green of coriander and garlic smeared over bread. Shisha was smoked, Hussaini started with a dance and poems, and then we all joined in, tales were told of the battles, songs were sung and old Janpath the Jain played surprisingly well. I mean, it was still awful but it was his best, interspersing notes with jokes of wrestling a British officer to the floor and firing on another from hundreds of metres away. We laughed, for Janpath was a Jain and what nonsense he spoke to cheer us. We danced and danced, tablas played and people fired their rifles in time. That night, me and Hussaini kissed in a quiet moment. Her eyes seemed to have a fire in them even when the candles had burned all the way down. We talked and talked.

The way people spoke, you would have thought the whole of India would have been ours again in weeks. We talked of what the future might look like. Of things being even better than they were even before the British. The zamindars and rulers would see that we were the ones who placed us back on the throne. They would reward us with land and I saw a world in which I would move to the banks the river. The banks of my childhood.

I had always known that even if she loved me, the cause of freedom came first. I wish I was as noble, if I could have convinced her I would have run away from the world with her. Found a small hut on the banks of the Ganges, immersed in a world of dark wood and bright green leaves, all reflected on the opaque water's surface. We would work the land and spend our spare time looking for kingfishers and butterflies. But that would have been wrong of me, she had a far higher purpose than my heart. For that reason I never told her I loved her. We kissed again and again and again and a song sang in my heart.

Officer   Sing it.

Rebel   What?

Officer   Sing the song that was in your heart.

Rebel   I am no singer.

Officer   I can tell much about soul from the way it sings. Sing. Anything. Sing the song which comes into your mind when you think of Hussaini.

Rebel *sings first verse of 'The Braes o' Balquhither'.*

Officer   Louder, please.

Rebel *continues to sing.*

Officer   Well, I won't lie, your singing could do with work. But I wasn't expecting that. You do know an old Highland song.

Rebel   Some officers have things genuinely worth trading.

Officer   My grandmother used to sing it to me. She thought of my grandfather when she sang. You must love your Hussaini very much.

Rebel *nods.*

Officer   And you never told her you loved her. Pity that. You want my honest opinion?

Rebel *is silent.*

Officer   I'll tell you. I don't know why you didn't have the strength to tell her. Maybe she would have shared those same dreams. Maybe you would be standing here knowing she loved you too.

Rebel   That is the first thing you have said which may have something to it.

Officer   So that is why you want to live. You want to see her again?

Rebel   I have heard nothing of her, I don't even know if she is alive.

Officer   But you believe that she must be. Amazing what love does to the mind. Bless you, my sweet lovestruck rebel, and hey, look at us, getting somewhere, eh! A bit of rapport. And I bet deep down you even liked the guitar.

Rebel   I didn't hate it.

Officer   She sounds like an interesting woman. Tell me, though. Why was she so passionate about throwing us off?

Rebel   Because she is a hijra and a tawaif and one who believes in what is right.

Officer   Sorry, a tawaif, isn't that a prostitute? Sex for money is a sin.

Rebel   Courtesan. And there is nothing sinful about it. Here sex is not something to be ashamed of. Tawaifs are respected, celebrated for so much more than sex, they are bastions of art and culture. They know poetry, dancing and many advise our most powerful.

Officer   Ha! Your great men advised by whores. I suppose that is why you were so easy to conquer.

Rebel   If they had been better heeded I am sure we would have never been conquered in the first place.

Officer   Ooh, touché. Now, tawaif I know. A hijra. What is that?

Rebel   A hijra, a woman who may have been mistaken for a man at birth, or perhaps born both man and woman. They are their own community, famed for their righteousness ever since they stood by Lord Rama, many millenia ago.

Officer   A man in women's clothes is wrong. As is a man loving another man. What you did is a sin in the eyes of God.

Rebel   They are not men.

Officer   Now, I will conceded I am not doctor. But as far as I am aware anyone with a wiggle, waggly, tallywacker is a man. No matter how much he wants to be otherwise.

Rebel   You think of me as a man, then?

Officer   You are one of these hijras? You could at least shave . . .

Rebel   No, I am not a hijra, nor am I a man. I am myself. It scares me what you are doing, demonising us, demonising her. That is why she wished to fight you, to protect her people and to protect all our people.

Officer   OK, you think me insensitive, but all I can see is a little cultural clash here. I am not against you. But I do think you are trying to say too many things at once. Don't want to over complicate the narrative.

Rebel   You agree it may be more complex?

Officer   Tell you what, the next one of these we do you could try and persuade me that there is more to gender and whores.

Rebel   Tawaifs.

Officer   Tawaifs. Than I think. And and I shan't comment on him or what you are anymore.

Rebel   Her.

Officer   Her, exactly.

Rebel   Next one of these?

Officer   Well, I think this is going really well? The song was quite a poignant moment and we have an unusual but compelling chemistry. We might get a follow up if it's well received.

Rebel   You planning on not lighting the fuse, then?

Officer   You going to tell me what I need to know?

Rebel   I am telling you what you need to know.

Officer   Then whaddya know, you will be out of here in no time. A happy ending for all. Where were we? You had taken Kanpur and were having a little kiss to celebrate?

Rebel   The kissing was short lived as a man called Tatya Tope, the general, called her over with a word.

Prisoners.

She went fast.

As well as masters of Kanpur, we were now masters of prisoners. Around a hundred of the Giant's soldiers and a couple of hundred of women and children.

Quickly, it was agreed that Wheeler, the Giant's man, and the other prisoners would be free to leave. Not long after, boats were arranged for the prisoners. Carts, dollies and even elephants were brought and we loaded the women, children and sick onto them. It was a time of reasonable good will, like two opponents having played a sports match and the winner attempting to be gracious. So much so that we let the British officers keep their ammunition and rifles.

When the day came, I walked side by side with a Giant's officer and his family. His wife and child actually seemed remarkably calm. The wife smiled and the child, she pulled faces at me. I pulled them back, making my eyes as wide as I could. There was fear in his eyes though. I wonder if he knew what plans they had for us if we had failed. If he knew the violence he and his division had already inflicted on our bodies and he was terrified we would do the same in return.

It was still summer, the banyan trees wilting brown in the heat. This was no time to look for kingfishers. With monsoon rains yet to wash away so much of the dust and muck, and so the river was unusually low. It made bringing the boats in tricky, getting people onto them even more so. The heat continued to build and tensions rose. Everything felt so on edge. Arguments between the British officers, forgetting they were not our masters anymore.

Then I don't know how it happened. The arguing was made silent by a single shot. Then a scream. I don't know who fired or who screamed first. Men from our side shouted a war cry and raced to the river bank. Rifles were loaded, fired, reloaded. The Giant's men raced to the edge of their boats doing the same. I saw bodies drop around me like fallen branches in a storm.

Suddenly, shots were flying above my head . . . I ducked for cover behind a tree trunk. Splinters flying around my ears as the bullets did too. And there was Hussaini, screaming at everyone to stop, I screamed for her to get down, but Hussaini just watched on. All I could see was the back of her head, eventually she went quiet I know not in horror, in disbelief or something else.

The rifles relentless until they weren't. A strange sudden silence and a false fog of gunpowder hung heavy in the air. In that fog, I did not see what happened to Wheeler's boat, further down the river. But I heard it. The sound of our rifles and the cries of British men, there was no armed response. Only misty silence once more.

The deal of safe passage had been broken.

Officer   Wheeler's boat had surrendered. That is why they weren't firing. You know that. Such a horrid trap you laid for them.

Rebel   It was no trap. If we wanted them dead, why wouldn't we have done it when we took the camp? Who lets a prisoner carry a rifle to fire back at their executioners? You haven't given such privileges since . . .

Officer   Enough of that. This is about you. And what your people did, if you can even be considered people after this.

Rebel   You speak of us as if we are animals! Before you came my people had wealth, not just in gold, but art and architecture, it was far from perfect but we had community too. Hindus, Muslims and Sikhs had never been more at odds with one another since your taking control.

Officer   Ohh come, come, it isn't like you were all la-de-da, flowers in your hair, holding hands and singing songs before we came here. Wasn't it Mughals who came up with this idea of blowing people up from cannons? Isn't the Mughal persecution of the Sikhs why the Sikhs didn't fight with you?

Rebel   We did not stand with them, I do not blame them for not standing with us. You know more than you let on.

Officer   I am not just a handsome face. Though, crucially, I am handsome. Look, any infighting between your religions is your own fault and nothing to do with us. I am not saying you are animals but you are lesser peoples with lesser religions, fighting over them and killing each other is just what you lot do.

Rebel   And you Christians have never fought wars with each other?

Officer   That is different; we have one right god, people just sometimes get confused about it. Your lot have like four thousand gods, and forty religions, it's bound to cause chaos. What is it with the one god many god thing anyway? It can't be both.

Rebel   Two things can be true at once. And you think our religion's violent? Jains won't even walk on the grass to protect the animals from their feet.

Officer   Now, that is overkill. Oh, so Jain wasn't the musician's name, it was his religion.

Rebel   Janpath was his name.

Officer   Ohh, from your story, he and the musician are one in the same. He was peaceful? Because according to my reports . . .

Rebel   He liked to tell tall tales in jest, you will recall. Janpath quite literally never hurt a fly.

Officer   Well, if that is true he is with God now. Take comfort, in that I am right.

Rebel   What makes you so sure your god is right.

Officer   Well, if he was wrong would we have come to rule you under his all seeing eyes.

Rebel   Did he give you the guns that conquered us?

Officer   Well, he must have wanted us to give it a shot.

Rebel   Rifle sharp wit, but I hope that my gods' sense of justice is kinder than yours.

Officer   I mean our lord is all forgiving so I don't think it gets kinder than that.

Rebel   Oh, are you like him, then? All forgiving?

Officer   Well, I wouldn't go that far, some things are unforgivable. Now, back to what happened after the boats, I think we have it now, lose the epithets and call the British people by our names. Speak the words of what you did, and let us see how stubborn you remain.

Rebel   Tatya was white hot with fury as to the prisoner release going wrong. But also steadfast in a new conviction, we couldn't keep the prisoners any longer. Nana Sahib mostly stayed silent. It seemed that his birthright to lead wasn't exactly much of a qualification for actually leading us. Hussaini argued that if the women and children who had lived were with us we had a duty of care for them. Tatya reluctantly agreed, but insisted they were kept to the Bibi Ghar or the House of the Ladies, but it was just a small building. Confined and cramped the women and children were living on top of each other. Days went by like this. I saw that British officer's family again. He had not survived what happened by the banks of the Ganga. But they had. The child tried to pull faces at me again and the mother pulled her away. I do not blame her.

More days went by and their conditions worsened. Squalid and with many of the prisoners wounded from the fight, illnesses broke out which caused more illness in turn. Hussaini kept arguing for better conditions but Tope argued it was poor strategy, we needed to fortify the city, there would be retribution for what we had done, and couldn't be worrying about them. I waited for Hussaini's eyes to blaze but they didn't. They had dimmed a little since the skirmish by the river.

And then news started to come in. A British force led by Havelock, your commanding general, and the 78th Highland Division, your division, was marching our way. Nana Sahib sent out two forces to prevent their advance and both were defeated. Hussaini had gone and came back with the second force. There were many times I had struggled to read her but this was the first time I ever saw doubt in her expression. Never short of words, she was silent for days.

Nana Sahib, who had prefered to say little over the last weeks announced. There were reports that Havelock, now unchecked, was simply burning down villages. Hanging indiscriminately. So much for the great British sense of justice. He said he had tried to use the prisoners in negotiations for our safety but Havelock was uninterested.

Now we too were cramped and suffocating under weight of the choices we faced. The palace halls which had once felt like they stretched to the skies now loomed over us. Janpath the Jain no longer played, horrified at how the women and children were being treated. We ate no kebab and biryani, only bland daal and rice.

Days more went by, all was frozen in the heat of the late rains. And then, more news. Havelock had raped and hanged one of Nana Sahibs own daughters.

And Tope saw his chance. If they were killing us, we must kill them. This was the price of freedom, and they did not deserve to live just so we should die. And Nana Sahib nodded. His wives said they would go on hunger strike. Janpath said he would never play again, that is why he wouldn't play for you, and Shaib was unmoved. I waited for Hussaini, we all waited for her, for her eyes to blaze to tell Tope that he was wrong, to say that we were a noble people and this was no way to prove it. But it didn't go that way.

Officer   And what did you say? Now is the moment to prove your innocence. What did you do?

Rebel   Nowhere near enough. I just stood there as Hussaini stormed out, saying she would care for the women and children, she emphasised those words. I couldn't think that these plans were right. Nor could I think they were wrong. Who was I to judge, what if I was weak willed, but this pride of freedom seemed so heavy. I walked down to the banks of the Ganga in the hope that she would provide an answer.

And an answer she did. I knew it in my heart of hearts. They were in our care and we had a duty to care for them. Havelock or not. I made a plan to seek out Hussaini, if I could rally her, if I could rally her she would be strong enough to oppose Tope and win round Sahib at least the day would be stayed if not saved.

But it did not go that way. On my way back to the encampment, I heard the sound of hoofbeats approaching fast and soon was staring down the barrel of two gleaming rifles silhouetted against bright red coats. One man was white, the other was brown. My heart fell at the sight of a brown man about to abduct me. He placed a bag over my head and intense pain came before a deeper darkness swiftly fell over my eyes.

Officer   Hm, so you really weren't there. I suppose I will have to tell you what comes next. Step back to the cannon, please. (**Rebel** *hesitates*.) If you do not I will have one of my officers shoot you, so it makes no difference. In fact, I cannot be sure they won't accidentally hit someone in the crowd first.

Rebel   You wouldn't.

Officer   They are tired with a battle they should have never had to fight, and which man doesn't find his aim wandering when he is tired. Now, please, this really is for your own good. I am still trying to help you. Trust me. Back to the cannon, for your sake and theirs.

(**Officer** *reties* **Rebel** *to cannon*.) So it is for the second time it is my turn to tell you a story. I told you you might learn something from me if you played your part right. I don't know how it happened, if you so claim it wasn't planned, it is hard to believe such deplorable violence wasn't. We arrived to liberate Kanpur and the palace as quick as we could as we knew you had the women and children held hostage. After Sahib surrendered he disappeared. Everything was undefended and your people looked at us like dogs who had done something deplorable. We called out for the women and children. Someone told us that they were inside the women's house, she was weeping with fear and then we ran.

I was one of the first in, the door stuck to the floor with blood. The place was literally running ankle deep in the red stuff, ladies' hair torn from their heads was lying about the floor; their poor little children's shoes lying here and there, gowns, frocks and bonnets belonging to these poor creatures scattered everywhere. But, to crown all the horrors, after they had been killed, all were thrown down a deep well in the compound. I looked down and saw them lying in heaps. I was told some were even thrown in alive. It is a sight which will never leave me.

That is what your people did. You must now see why I struggle to see you as people like us, in a way it is easier to be merciful if I see some of you as animals. You are not on the right side of this. I have heard your story and think you innocent of this specific crime. But I think now, you know the truth of your peoples actions, that you will tell me where Tatya and Nana Sahib went. I think you will condemn them and I think you will beg for forgiveness from me and my God. Then, once Sahib and Tope are brought to justice, I will be satisfied and only when I am satisfied will you walk away alive.

Rebel   You think I didn't hear?! While you left me to rot without food or water, you think the walls did not talk. Do you not think I heard?

Officer   Look here!

Rebel   Let me speak on my own terms! If this is to be my end I will no longer bend double, knees buckling under the weight of your desire to make a story for your ears. This isn't just a story, this isn't myth or legend, it is my life. It is our people's lives. We are people. And you call us animals, you end your tale after my people cause harm, which I do not deny. Yet omit what yours did next? You think I didn't hear

how you and your men flooded our streets, beat us, raped
us, burned our villages, burned living bodies, rounded us up
like swine and cattle, force fed Hindus beef and Muslims
pork and then hung them respectively in pig skins and in
cow skins, and you suddenly so culturally aware call us
animals, you strapped us to cannons, blew us to smitherines
in front of crowds forced to watch? You murdered old
Janpath the Jain the same way. His body in pieces, he will
never have his burial rights. This too is to be my fate and if
we are animals then you are butchers. Butchers who
somehow are shocked at the sight of the blood. How can you
be shocked at the sight of blood, when you waded ankle deep
into Kanpur in the red stuff of my friends? How can you be
shocked at the sight of blood when you have killed so many?
When you forced my people to lick the blood from the Bibi
Ghar and from the boots of your officers? When you stand
in the blood of old Janpath in the sand and say it will simply
be washed away by the rains that will not come? And for
what? Justice? Revenge? Call punishment what it is.

We didn't dream of this. We dreamt of a future, one where
life would not be perfect but it would be ours to live.

Laughs.

Officer   How can you laugh?

Rebel   How can I not? A cabin by the banks of the Ganga,
looking for kingfishers again, you have cut down the trees,
the kingfishers long since dead, what future,

Officer   There is no future for you if you carry on like this.

Rebel   Ohh, I see a future. Where you rule us with an iron
fist to our guts and boots on our necks. Where millions of us
will live under the trigger of your gleaming rifles and grand
explosions. Where no matter how peacefully we ask for
freedom you will respond with bullets. And if we respond
with bullets of our own you will cry in horror. I do not deny
that we have killed your people. How many of us will bring
just one of yours back? How many brown lives is a white life

worth? How different can white skin make a human being? How can you think you are right in this?

Officer   I don't think anyone is in a position to question me after what you did to my people. You speak as if you can justify it.

Rebel   I am not trying to justify it. I weep for those who died in our hands, it was wrong.

Officer   There. You said it. You said. You said it was wrong. You admit it was wrong. Is that not condemnation?

Rebel   Two things can be true at once. It was wrong, but what if –

Officer   For the love of goodness speak sense, man.

Rebel   I am not a man. I am not an animal. I am a human being. And I cannot make sense of this senseless world, let alone speak it. For me it, the killing, was wrong but who am I to judge the actors? Perhaps Tope is right and I am weak? Perhaps it should have never come to pass. If only Hussaini were here she would . . .

Officer   Did you not hear of your beloved Hussaini?

Rebel   What news? Why didn't you say earlier.

Officer   She has disappeared. But according to your own she was no fine advisor, nor a freedom fighter. But a depraved beast. The lowest of the low. They say she was made to care for the women and children. And she forced the sepoys to fire upon and hired butchers to finish the job when they stopped from weeping.

Rebel   Hussaini would have never.

Officer   Not my people's words. Yours. They are blaming her. She, in fact, is the one they want the most.

Rebel   Don't you see. This is how it starts. Your people demonize her and mine turn on her and . . .

Officer   She is not yet found. I believe your story. You are both innocent, there I have said it, but to prove it we must, you must give them up. Someone must answer for these sins. In giving them up, you will save her and save yourself. You must trust me.

Rebel   You knew this whole time, of what happened to her, you knew everything and yet you played the fool, and now you expect me to trust you to save her life.

Officer   Both of your lives, I played the fool to gain your trust, I admit it. Look, we have been like two gladiators locked in combat. I'll admit the odds were always in my favour, so I'll take no great triumph in my victory, and therefore you, so obdurate and proud, are noble in defeat. Victory and defeat shall come in condemnation and revelation. I always sought to save you and now I have your story I will seek to save Hussaini. I only threatened the crowd as I knew that the cannon was needed to get your confession. It was a game, all of this, every twist and turn a game to bring the words I needed from your lips. And I have won. I shall be the gracious victor and embrace you, my cannon-bound friend, and in doing so show that the British man still loves his Indian servant. Is capable of forgiveness for Indians if they shall only agree to better themselves. Now, you said you were one who always watches and never acts, now is your chance to change that. Come, condemn them, speak just a few words of Shaib and Tope and better yourself, save your life, save her life and have our happy ending . . . come, friend, speak. Come, friend, speak . . . Come, friend, speak. For God's sake, let me save you.

Rebel   You cannot save me.

Officer   You would risk Hussaini's life for your stubborn pride?

Rebel   If she is not found, she is safer without me. I have my news.

Officer   Forget her, then. Save yourself.

Rebel Why does my life matter to you?

Officer Because an innocent soul cannot be killed like this.

Rebel If old Janpath was not innocent enough to live then nor am I.

Officer Ohh, stop this. You admit it was wrong but won't condemn them. How many times must I ask you to speak simple words?

Rebel And how many times must I ask you, what makes you think you are right?

Officer Because it has to be right. Because I have to be right. What we have done, all of it, has to be right, or else the wrong is unimaginable. I cannot save them, those who must die. I could not save the Jain musician, his false boasting and jangling keys upon the cannon killed him. And I will not save them, Sahib and Tope, those who deserve death for their wrongs. But you don't deserve death, not like this. Just condemn them and then the day will be stayed at least. Everyone has a part to play and you said, everything is a story we tell. You wrote it. You are the one who is telling it.

Rebel And yet you are the one who decides how it ends!

Officer No friend, I am not, why throw your life away?

Rebel I am not the one who strapped me to a cannon, friend. You speak as if I bound my hands myself, lit the fuse with my hands bound and as if I will smile when the cannonball shattered and spatters my body. My body in pieces, I will never have my burial rights. Were it any different, I would do differently. But I will not betray all I hold dear just to live. If this is a choice then I make it. Know I do not wish to die, I do not choose death. But, I cannot judge them, I am not a god, mine or yours, I cannot reveal them. If condemnation is required it will come from my people for my people, but here and now, you must decide what happens next.

Officer   This isn't how it was supposed to go. I needed more time. (*Cannot say sorry.*) God forgive me. (**Officer** *walks off stage.*)

Rebel   Where are you going? Stay and finish it, then. How long till the fuse goes off? Will you spare me anyway? You are silent? After so much talk? What more would you have me say? You have the story. In your eyes I may be innocent. In the eyes of your people I can only be innocent or guilty. In my own, I am both and neither. I do not wish to die. I wish to live. I wish to see the tall trees line the banks of the Ganga once more, to hear the sound of the kingfisher on the banks, to catch a glimpse of its blue and orange blaze, to see her one last time, to tell Hussaini, to tell her what I never told her, to tell her, I lo–

Cannon goes off.

Projection end titles   *It is estimated that tens of thousands if not hundreds of thousands of Indians were killed in response to the events at Kanpur.*

Hussaini, *after being blamed for the murders, disappears from the historical record.*

Tatya Tope *fought with other forces until succumbing in the years that followed.*

Nana Sahib *disappeared entirely, presumed dead or in hiding.*

'Remember Kanpur' became a rallying cry for the British army across the empire.

A monument to fallen 78th Highland Division soldiers still stands outside Edinburgh Castle.

Ten years later it was made illegal to be a hijra.

They did not regain legal recognition of their gender until 2014.

Following the Uprising, India experienced another ninety years of British rule, enduring extortion, famine and regular massacres, before finally being granted independence in 1947.

End of piece.